Take Con

Personal Money Management

A practical guide for managing household income and saving money

Peter Dickinson

Table of Contents

Acknowledgements

This guide is dedicated to all volunteers and staff who work tirelessly to support, assist and advise people in their time of need.

Volunteers and staff of Pembrokeshire Citizens Advice, who supported me during my fledgling years as a volunteer advisor, Recruitment Coordinator, Trainer and Financial Capability Coordinator.

All Financial Capability trainers and advisers, who continue to empower people to take control of their personal finances.

Citizens Advice UK, Money & Pensions Service, Turn2Us, National Debt Line and StepChange, for providing the general public with Free access to support, guidance and information, without favour and regardless of circumstance.

Martin Lewis 'Money Saving Expert', for raising the profile of 'personal money management', and his commitment to campaign for financial justice.

Welsh Government and Pembrokeshire County Council for their support in the delivery of free financial capability advice to the residents of Pembrokeshire.

Finally, my parents John and Kakena, children Shelley, Andrew (deceased), Jodie and Matthew, Aunts Cetta and Christine, for their love, support and guidance that humbles me every day.

About the author.

Peter Dickinson is a retired Police officer, having served 32 years with Dyfed Powys Police in Mid and West Wales.

Following retirement from the Police in 2010, Peter commenced volunteering with Pembrokeshire Citizens Advice.

In April 2013, Peter was given ownership of a new 'Financial Capability' project.

Together with his administration assistant, Bhavani Athithan and volunteers Emma Beaumont, Tatiana Sheremeta, Philippa Cole and Robert John, Peter developed training material and commenced delivery of group sessions throughout the county.

The content was tailored for each group, e.g. students, retired, unemployed, low income earners and parents; and included, Problem Debt, Budgeting, Smart Shopping, Bank Accounts, Saving & Borrowing and Domestic Energy. The demand from learners, for individual, face to face advice, grew and became the mainstay of his work.

In June 2015, on behalf of Citizens Advice UK, Peter launched the West Wales Financial Capability Forum; a quarterly meeting of front-line workers, where best practice and new initiatives are shared. The West Wales Area of Wales Financial Capability Forum still exists, under the stewardship of William Jones and Geraldine Murphy.

In April 2016, in order to continue with the funding, Peter was obliged to become self-employed and set up Fincap Training Solutions, as a sole trader.

Peter continues to deliver free advice and group sessions to the residents of Pembrokeshire, thanks to the support of Pembrokeshire County Council and Welsh Government.

Peter also works with Coleg sir Gar, delivering free online training sessions to unemployed adults at Job Centre Plus and Careers Wales offices throughout Pembrokeshire.

Introduction

Money doesn't buy you happiness, but that doesn't mean it's not important.

There are many quotes about the value of money, but one that I believe has an impactive practical resonance was written by American radio host and author David Ramsey.

"You must gain control over your money, or the lack of it will forever control you".

Regardless of how much or how little money you have, it is what you do with it that matters.

Not having enough money to pay basic bills is an awful experience to go through; but living beyond your means can result in an ongoing feeling of anxiety and may cause severe illness.

Our relationship with money is developed and shaped during childhood. Like most things, we learn from our family and peer group. There is very little external influence to guide us and we invariably learn from our mistakes later in life.

We are all individuals, living in circumstances that are unique to us, but we all have things that we *like* to spend money on and things that we *do not like* to, but cannot avoid.

My personal pet hate is 'car parking charges'. I find myself muttering with contempt every time I have to pay my local authority for the privilege of parking my car, so that I can do my weekly shop at the local supermarket.

My work as a Financial Capability tutor has enabled me to assist many people to take control of their finances and have more money to spend on the things that they *like* spending it on.

In this short guide I will share with you, simple processes to help you stay in control and develop the knowledge to improve your financial situation.

The Carrot

Before we go any further, I need to grab your attention.

So how would you like some free money?

Cashback websites are real, genuine, easy to use and they pay you money when you shop.

Let me give you an example – you need to buy a mobile phone.

You can buy the phone, (contract or PAYG, it does not matter), from a shop in the High Street e.g. Carphone Warehouse, EE, Vodaphone. You walk into the shop, choose your phone, hand over your cash, complete the purchase and leave with your new device; or

You can visit the same store online, make exactly the same purchase, hand over the same amount of money, complete your purchase and receive it by post within a couple of days; or

You can join a *Cashback website*, visit the same online store using a link from the Cashback website, make exactly the same purchase, pay exactly the same money, get exactly the same product delivered to your door **AND they give you money**.

Honestly, there is no catch, this is free money, simply for buying things you were going to buy anyway.

And it is not just mobiles, Insurance, electricals, clothes, shoes, furniture, travel ……..the list goes on! Please be patient, all will be revealed.

Overview.

Financial Capability

Having a level of understanding of financial matters to effectively achieve individual and family financial goals.

Financial Inclusion

A state where all people have access to appropriate, desired financial products and services in order to manage their money effectively. It is achieved by financial capability on the part of the consumer and availability of products on the part of suppliers.

Financial Exclusion

A state where individuals cannot access the financial products that they need. This may be due to lack of knowledge or access on behalf of the consumer or disproportionate eligibility criteria on behalf of the suppliers.

Taking Control

There are four areas that you need to review, in order to take control of your personal finances:

1. Problem Debt – if you have problem debt it needs to be sorted.
2. Budgeting – in its simplest terms Income v Expenditure.
3. Smart shopping – cashback, value for money & best deals.
4. Bank Accounts, Saving & Borrowing – identify best products.

We will take a look at each area in turn.

However, in order to successfully take control of your personal finances they must be reviewed in this order.

Chapter One

Problem Debt.

First of all, you need to realise that not all debt is bad.

Good Debt

Good debt is an investment, at the cheapest possible rate, that will grow in value or generate long-term income.

Examples are: Mortgage to buy property, Student Loan to gain a qualification that could help gain employment at higher salary, car loan to buy a car that enables you to gain employment.

Bad Debt

Bad debt is 'unaffordable' borrowing, commonly taken out to make unnecessary purchases, or to pay existing debt, especially when high interest rates are charged.

Debt becomes a Problem when it is no longer manageable.

Even a good debt can become a problem debt when your circumstances change, and what was once affordable becomes a concern.

Changes in circumstance can include loss of employment, reduction in hours, family breakdown, illness, increase in household (babies, new relationships) ….. again, the list goes on.

Some signs of 'problem debt' are:

using credit card for cash advances & only paying off minimum amount, going without food or heating in order to pay credit instalments, borrowing more to pay existing debt. Feeling sick in the stomach at every knock on the door, or when the mail is delivered.

Whatever the reason for it, problem debt must be managed as soon as possible.

Ignoring the problem will make you anxious and could make you ill.

You have to *Take control* and deal with it.

But you do not have to do it alone.

Professional help is available & it's FREE.

Whilst all Problem debt has to be dealt with, some debts are more important than others.

Priority Debts

A priority debt is one which if not paid or managed, can lead to serious consequences such as imprisonment, loss of home or having a service/supply disconnected.

So, if you have multiple creditors, you need to identify which ones are Priority Debts.

Here are some examples:

Priority	Non-priority
Rent / Mortgage	Mobile phone
Gas	Catalogue
Electricity	Water
Council Tax	Credit cards
Magistrates Court Fines	Unsecured personal loan
Child Support	Bank Overdraft
Secured Personal Loan	Store cards

Golden Rules to take control of Problem debt.

- Acknowledge the problem,
- Contact creditors as soon as possible and let them know you are seeking help,
- Seek help.

There are several organisations that can help, with Specialist debt advisors who will not judge you.

The most difficult thing for you, is to make that first contact.

Charitable Organisations that can help.

Free – Independent – Impartial - Confidential

Citizens Advice.

This is an organisation that was founded on 4th September 1939 (the day after the outbreak of World War 2) primarily to assist with the loss of ration books, homelessness, evacuation, and the location of missing persons. Nowadays, volunteers and staff working within locally based charities, assist people with all sorts of problems, including *Problem Debt*.

You can contact your local office by email, telephone or arrange a face to face appointment.

https://www.citizensadvice.org.uk/   03444 77 20 20

The Citizens Advice Website offers self-help information and advice plus a search facility to find your nearest office.

National Debt Line

Online and telephone advice

https://www.nationaldebtline.org/   0808 808 4000

StepChange

Online and telephone advice

https://www.stepchange.org/   0800 138 1111

Money Advice Service (aka Money & Pensions Service)

This organisation was set up by Government, but is also Free & Impartial, offering online and telephone advice

https://www.moneyadviceservice.org.uk/ 0800 138 7777

Debt Remedies

Professional debt advisors are trained to provide you with the best advice for your situation. The first thing the advisor will do is to check that you are liable for the debt and that it must be repaid.

You might not have to pay a debt if:

- it has been six years or more since you made a payment or were in contact with the creditor,
- there was a problem when you signed the agreement, for example if you were pressured into signing it or the agreement was not clear,
- the creditor did not check properly that you could afford the repayments when you signed the agreement.

If the advisor establishes that you are liable for the debt(s), there will be a discussion to ascertain your options. This will take account of things like the amount and type of debts you have, and how much money you can pay towards them.

Options include: Partial write off, Debt Management Plan (DMP), Administrative Order, Individual Voluntary Arrangement (IVA), Debt Relief Order (DRO) and Bankruptcy. These are complex matters that will impact on your future credit worthiness.

I cannot stress enough the importance of seeking Professional Help.

If you do not deal with your problem debts, your creditor(s) may take formal action against you.

Depending on the type of debt, they could instruct Bailiffs (Enforcement Officers) or issue Court Proceedings.

Bailiffs - Enforcement Officers

If you receive a letter, 'notice of enforcement' from a Bailiff, do not ignore it. *Contact your local Citizens Advice for help*. If you ignore the letter, a Bailiff may turn up at your door, which may incur fees that will be added to your debt.

If a Bailiff turns up at your door, unless the debt is for an unpaid Magistrates Court Fine or to HMRC, they cannot force entry. That being said 'forced entries' are normally only carried out as a final recourse and by using a locksmith not a battering ram.

If the debt is for anything else, **do not let them in**. If you are expecting a Bailiff to call, make sure that everyone in the household knows not to let them in. Speak to them through a window or closed door and if they need to hand you documents, they can be posted through the letterbox.

Also make sure that when you go out, all doors are locked, and windows closed. A Bailiff, with the proper paperwork, can legally enter a property through an unlocked door.

Do not let it get this far – get help.

Chapter Two

Budgeting

When problem debt is under control or if you do not have problem debt, the next area to review is Budgeting.

In its simplest terms, budgeting is managing your expenditure based on income.

You need to decide which time frame to use, based upon how often you receive your income.

This will usually be either weekly, fortnightly or monthly.

Income

Sources of regular household income are quite limited – the main ones being salary, welfare benefits, pension, dividends, child support, interest from savings and rents from property owned.

Income Maximisation is an important process that should be conducted to ensure that you are not missing out on monies due to you.

If you are employed, check that you are earning at least the minimum wage.

https://www.gov.uk/national-minimum-wage-rates

If you are entitled to incremental pay increases check that you have received them.

Check your tax code to make sure you are not paying too much income tax or if you are owed a rebate.

https://www.gov.uk/income-tax-rates

If you receive welfare benefits, check that you are getting your full entitlement.

Citizens Advice can help you to do this.

Another Charitable Organisation – **Turn2Us** can also help. They have an online benefit calculator that will identify what you should be receiving.

https://benefits-calculator.turn2us.org.uk/AboutYou

They also have a particularly useful tool that allows you to check if you are eligible to apply for a grant:

https://grants-search.turn2us.org.uk/

Expenditure

Once you have established your regular income, you need to review your expenditure.

Regular essential household bills can be broken down into five headings:

Rent / Mortgage

Council Tax

Gas / Electric

Water

Child Support

Make a written record of how much each bill is and on what date it is due.

We will look at ways to reduce your gas / electric / water bills in the

'Smart Shopping' section.

If you use **cash** to pay these bills then physically take the money from your income and put it in a safe place for when it is needed. This is commonly referred to as 'jam jar' budgeting, but most people use envelopes not jam jars!

If you pay by **Direct Debit** from your bank, make sure that there are sufficient funds to cover them.

If you use a **payment card**, make sure that you keep up with regular payments.

Whichever time frame for budgeting you use (weekly, monthly or fortnightly):

Calculate the sum: INCOME minus TOTAL REGULAR BILLS

This will leave you with an amount of money for '**Other Expenditure**'.

In order to accurately convert income or expenditure from annual to monthly to weekly, use the following calculations:

Annual to Monthly – divide by 12

Monthly to Annual – multiply by 12

Annual to Weekly – divide by 52

Weekly to Annual – multiply by 52

Monthly to Weekly – multiply by 12 then divide by 52

Weekly to Monthly – multiply by 52 then divide by 12

Other expenditure

Other expenditure, can be placed into broader categories, such as:

Food

Clothing

Telephone / Broadband / TV

Travel (private car / public service / taxi)

Toiletries / cleaning materials

Children activities

Socialising

Pets

Holidays

Insurance

Debt (Credit cards / Personal Loans / Overdraft)

Savings

This is not a finite list, there are far more ways of spending money than bringing it in!!

Managing your remaining money to spend on 'other expenditure' is one of the hardest things to gain control over.

There are two principles that can help you to choose how to do this.

Needs -vs- Wants & **Prioritising.**

Needs -vs- Wants

Notwithstanding that we are all different, there are some things that we need to survive and other things that we would simply like to have for enjoyment.

We need food, clothing, water, heat, and shelter; but there are many ways to achieve these things, all at different costs.

We do not *need* to eat lobster and steak regularly even though we might *want* to.

We do not *need* to buy designer clothing, even though we might *want* to always look trendy.

We do not *need* to have a bath every night, even though we might *want* a soak before bed.

We do not *need* the most expensive mobile phone to stay in contact with family/friends, even though we really *want* to have the latest gadgets.

We do not *need* the heating on all day, because we do not *want* to wear extra layers of clothing.

We do not *need* to live in a large property, even though we might *want* to have lots of room and a big garden.

Whenever you are thinking about making a purchase, ask yourself if you really **need** it. If you do not' but still really **want** it, then you have to ask yourself, *"can I afford to buy it, without leaving me short for the other things I need?"*.

If the answer is yes – then go ahead and enjoy your purchase.

If the answer is no – then wait until you are in a position to answer yes.

Wants are things that we do not need but would really like to have, the large TV, full SKY package, foreign holiday, bigger car, that extra present for the kids, hot tub …… this list is endless.

It is not a bad thing to want stuff – but you should only buy them if you can afford to, without going into problem debt or taking money out of the **'Needs'** budget.

Prioritising

There will be occasions when you have identified a number of things that you need/want to spend your money on, but the stark reality is that you cannot afford them all.

You have to 'prioritise' and only spend what you can afford.

You have to make choices, sometimes this will be easy but occasionally it will be more difficult.

Consider these two lists and think about how you would place the items in each one in order of importance.

List 1	List 2
Transport / fuel	Your 6yrs old child needs new shoes
Sky / Netflix / Amazon	You owe a friend some money
Food / Clothes	Gas bill is due
Rent / Mortgage	You have a job interview – need haircut
Mobile phone	A jacket you want is 70% off in the sale
Gas / Electric / Oil	The rent/mortgage payment is due
	Food is getting low – need to shop
	Partner's birthday – need a present

There are no right or wrong answers because we all have different circumstances, but some things will be more important to you than others.

Grocery Shopping

If I asked you "How much is your monthly grocery shop?", you may have a rough idea; but would you know how much of that amount is for bread, or milk, or chocolate or crisps?

The only true way to identify what you spend on groceries is to keep ALL receipts and **make a record**.

This can be a paper record or an electronic one on a computer/laptop/tablet.

An example is shown below:

Date	Bread	Milk	Meat	Fruit	Vegetables	Biscuits

The first column is always for the date of the purchase, the columns to the right will be as many as there are different items in your shopping; and it must include ALL purchases.

If you buy a bar of chocolate with your pint of milk from the corner shop, or when you put fuel in the car, or whilst waiting for the bus – **record it**.

Do this for a month – and include everyone in your household.

You must be honest and for this to work, and you must shop as normal.

Do not reduce your outgoings or only buy healthy in order to look good. You will only be fooling yourself.

After the month, gather the household together and discuss the findings.

Are there certain things you could cut down on to save money?

Tips for grocery shopping.

- Plan meals write a list and stick to it!
- Do not shop when you are hungry.
- Shop without the children if possible!
- Eye-level products are the most profitable - look around and do not be fooled by expensive brand names.
- Buy non-perishables in bulk and when on offer.
- Check unit prices (e.g. price per kilo) - prices can vary a lot!
- Stick to a budget by using cash not card.

Branded -vs- Basic

There is a lot of competition for our business, we all know the budget food stores and the 'so called' premium ones.

Each store will be selling branded goods as well as their own brands.

As an individual you have to choose where you shop and which items you buy, this should not only be based upon cost but also taste and health.

It is pointless buying cheap tomato ketchup if nobody likes it. Experiment with different brands to find what is right for you; do not forget to check for salt and sugar content.

Take a look at the list of groceries below (prices correct on 23rd May 2020):

Branded	Item	Basic
Heinz £0.75	Baked beans 420 gms	Tesco £0.29
Heinz £2.70	Ketchup 700 gms	Tesco £0.84
Andrex £4.45	Toilet roll – 9 pack	Aldi £2.09
McVities £1.50	Chocolate Biscuits	Asda £0.60
Walls £2.10	Thick sausages (8)	Asda £1.70

Just on these 5 items the difference in price is £11.50 - £5.52 = £5.98

That is a saving of a whopping 52%

Higher price does not always mean better quality.

Special offers

Supermarkets will always try and tempt us with special offers, and sometimes it is a good idea to take advantage of them, but not always.

Have you ever bought the largest multipack of crisps because it was on offer?

Did it last any longer than normal, or did you just eat more crisps?

What is the best deal - buy one get one free or 50% off?

You may think they are the same, but they are not.

Check your shopping list – you wanted *one* particular item that costs £5.00.

With the 'special offer', you can now buy *two* of them for £5.00 – which is ok if you can afford it and it is non-perishable OR

You can buy the *one* that you wanted for £2.50 and have the other £2.50 to keep or spend on something else.

It is your choice, make it wisely.

Seeing is believing - bizarre pricing - check out this photo

McVities Jaffa Cakes, as seen on display in a Tesco store.

Pack of 12 - £1.19   Pack of 24 - £2.19   **Pack of 36 - £1.50**

28

The principles reflected upon in relation to grocery shopping can be repeated for all of the different areas of 'other expenditure'.

Suffice to say that if you look in detail at your current spending habits you may be able to modify them help manage your budget better.

Chapter Three

Smart Shopping

Your shopping habits will primarily depend on what you enjoy doing and how much you trust technology.

Before the dawn of the Internet, we all shopped in the High Street and some people still prefer to do this; however the frugal shopper will most definitely use the Internet to compare items and will usually complete the purchase online.

High Street -vs- Internet

Shopping on the *High Street* is a social experience, enjoyed by many and for some people is their only means of contact with other people.

However, the variety of choice depends on where you live and how far you want to travel.

The *Internet,* on the other hand, offers local, national, and international shopping from the comfort of your own home. Plus, the opportunity to compare prices offered by a variety of retailers.

The *High Street* experience allows you try out things in real time, especially clothing and footwear; and will invariably include a refreshment break of coffee or lunch.

Shopping *online* does not have to be a solo experience, but usually is however there are the benefits of your own toilet and refreshments on hand at a fraction of the cost. Plus, you will not get wet if the weather takes a turn for the worse!

Many people use a mix of both options, comparing items online, then going to the High Street store to try them out. Or looking at a product in store to check out colour, size etc, then making a cheaper online purchase.

We are all individuals and will do what suits us best.

If making an online purchase, consider the 'returns policy' to check if you will have to pay additional postage.

Online purchases should only ever be made on secure websites.

A secure website will start https://www and have a picture of a padlock.

Cashback Websites

As mentioned previously, cashback websites really are a no brainer and will pay you money (cash into your bank/PayPal account or enhanced vouchers), simply for shopping via their links.

You can even register a payment card and then collect cashback if you shop on the High Street.

The two main cashback websites are **Quidco** and **TopCashback**.

Quidco has two levels of account, a free one and a Premium one that has an annual administration fee of £5. The Premium account pays out a higher level of cashback, so is the one that I recommend you join.

TopCashback only has the one account, charging a £5 annual administration fee.

The two sites are in competition with each other and offer different amounts of cashback from the same retailers.

So why not join both and make as much free cash as you can.

Both sites also offer referral bonuses. So, if you use either or both of the below links, we will both get a referral bonus when you make your first purchase.

https://www.quidco.com/raf/185601/

https://www.topcashback.co.uk/ref/drooker687

Once your account is up and running, you will get a referral code of your own and can share it with family and friends.

You can of course join either site without using the links, just visit:

www.quidco.com or www.topcashback.co.uk

So how do they work?

Below you will see screenshots of both website home pages.

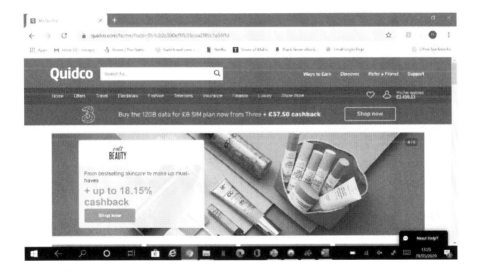

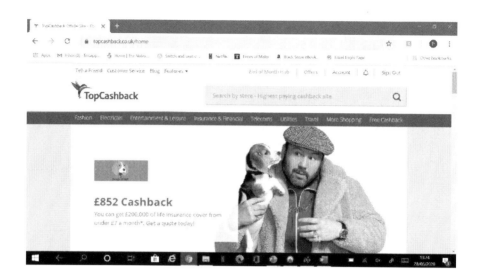

On both sites you will see a search box in which you can input the name of a retailer (Carphone Warehouse, Next, Currys, Argos, Lloyds Bank, etc) and click search. You will be taken to a results page which lists your chosen retailer, plus some of the competition; and will give an indication of the amount of cashback available. Click on the retailer, you will be taken to a page that shows in more detail the cashback available and links that say, **'get cashback'**. Click on the 'get cashback' link and you will be redirected to the retailer's own website.

Once on the retailer website, you shop as normal. If you complete a purchase you will receive an email saying that your cashback is being **'tracked'**.

Different retailers track at different speeds, some weeks, some months, but eventually you will receive an email saying that your cashback has been '**confirmed**'. At this point you can withdraw your '**free money**'.

When you set up your account you will be asked to provide bank or PayPal details, some people worry about this, that is why I left my Quidco account open when I took the screenshot. They want these payment details so that **they can pay money in**, not take it out.

You will also get the option to take High Street vouchers instead of cash, the value of the voucher will be enhanced up to 15% of the cash value.

If you do not know what store you are looking for, you can click on one of the topic headings – fashion, electricals, finance, insurance etc. The cashback amount will vary from a specific sum, e.g. £30, £50, £120 or a % of the sale price (please note it is the sale price ex vat).

My Eureka moment.

In November 2007, my home buildings and contents insurance policy was with Lloyds Bank (a condition of my mortgage). My renewal was due at a price of £400, which I considered a bit high. I went online to Lloyds Bank Insurance and was quoted £200 for exactly the same cover. Fortunately, I had recently been made aware of Quidco, but to be honest with you, I was sceptical about it so had not joined. I browsed the site and saw that buildings and contents insurance with Lloyds Bank offered a cashback of £120.

So, I joined Quidco, visited Lloyds Bank Insurance via the link, bought the £200 policy and three months later I received £120 cashback.

I was convinced!

Domestic Energy & Water

Gas and Electricity

One area where ongoing savings can be made is with Gas and Electricity.

You can make savings by being more efficient and using less, but you can also make savings by ensuring that you are on the best deal for your circumstances.

Energy companies charge us for the number of units (kWh) we use plus a daily standing charge for each meter.

Energy companies do not charge the same rates and there are dozens of them, each having multiple tariffs!

At the time of writing, the price of a unit of **Electricity** can vary between **47.53 pence and 12.60 pence**; the unit price of **Gas** can vary between **35.61 pence and 2.07 pence**.

The **daily standing charge** can vary between **37.67 pence and zero**.

Payment method.

The way you pay will also affect your ability to make savings.

There are two types of meter **PAYG** (prepayment) & **Credit**. Both of these can be either **SMART** or **DUMB**.

So, let us look at each in turn.

Pay as you go, or **Prepayment** meters are those where you top up a key or a card and insert into the meter. You pay in advance for what you are going to use. If you have a SMART meter you can top up with a mobile app or online to save you going out to your local PayPoint, Payzone or Post Office.

Credit meters allow you to pay for your energy after you have used it. These meters have displays showing a number known as a 'reading'. As you use your energy the number increases, and your usage is calculated by subtracting the previous reading from the current one. If you have a SMART meter your readings are automatically sent to your provider over the mobile phone network. If you have a DUMB meter then the readings have to read manually. If the energy provider does not have a current reading at the time of preparing a bill they will estimate your usage.

So, does it matter which type of meter you have?

Credit meters offer a huge choice of tariffs and because there is good competition between energy providers, the customer can choose the best deal for their circumstances.

If you do not take action to choose a **fixed rate** tariff (more on that later), you will by default be on your provider's **most expensive, standard** tariff. To qualify for a credit meter, you have to pass a *credit check*.

You use your energy in advance and can pay by Direct Debit (monthly or quarterly), upon receipt of a bill (quarterly) or with a payment card.

Prepayment meters are generally used by people on lower incomes and usually for one of five reasons:

1. I rent my home and the landlord insists that I have one,
2. I prefer this type of meter because it helps with my budgeting, if I cannot afford to top up then I go without,
3. I used to have a credit meter but got into arrears and the energy company said I had to change my meter,
4. My income is fortnightly, so I cannot guarantee money in my account on a fixed date to set up a direct debit,
5. I have a poor credit rating, so it is pointless asking for a credit meter.

Well guess what?

Prepayment tariffs are more expensive than Credit meter tariffs.

So, let us have a look at the five reasons above.

1. I can understand landlords being reluctant to allow a tenant to have a credit meter, because if the tenant gets into arrears, **it used to be**, that the property & the tenant were tagged with a bad credit marker; but that is no longer the case. It is only the tenant that is affected by the arrears. So, if this is 'your reason', have a word with your landlord.
2. I cannot argue with this reasoning; however, you need to do a comparison (again more on this a bit later) and see what savings can be made by switching to a credit meter. If you can save £20 a

month then maybe you should reconsider and focus a bit more on budgeting.

3. Past arrears may mean that your credit score is not too good, but time and better money management may have improved it; also the Energy Companies are legally bound to consider other options before insisting on a change to a Prepayment meter. If this did not happen then it is worth seeking advice.

4. This is one of the most common reasons I have encountered, but most energy companies will allow you to use a payment card, to pay an agreed monthly amount but not on a set date.

5. Even if you do have a poor credit rating, it is worth asking your energy provider the question. If you have regularly topped up your prepayment meter, they may look favourably at your situation.

Tariffs

A tariff is the name given to the plan you are on; this plan will identify the cost per unit of energy and rate of the daily standing charge. It will also have either an open ended 'variable' or **fixed term** of contract. Fixed term means that the price will be fixed until a specified date or period of time. Variable means that the price can change, either up or down depending on external factors, like the price of oil.

Energy companies will normally only have one **Prepayment** tariff, although they may charge a different rate if you have a Smart meter.

On 1st April 2017, the Government introduced a **Prepayment Meter Price Cap**. This cap is currently reviewed every six months (at the time of writing, the next review is 7th August 2020, with new price to take effect on 1st October 2020).

Since the introduction of the price cap, all Energy providers charge roughly the same and there is not much incentive to switch providers.

However, there is no harm in checking (see comparisons below).

Credit meter customers, on the other hand have access to a much wider choice of tariff, and huge savings can be made. All energy providers will offer several '**fixed**' rate tariffs alongside their default tariff, commonly referred to as a '**standard**' tariff..

'Standard' is the most expensive tariff available, and it makes no sense whatsoever for anyone to be on it.

Comparisons

There are dozens of energy providers competing for your business. A term often used in the domestic energy sector is 'the big six'.

The 'big six' energy companies are **British Gas, SSE, E.ON UK, EDF Energy, Scottish Power and npower**.

According to Government figures, these six companies provide approximately **7 out of every 10** British homes with gas and electricity.

So, with dozens of companies, each with several tariffs, how do you find the best one for your circumstances & how easy is it to switch?

You may be familiar with some commercial comparison sites, from national advertising. There are several comparison sites that can compare the domestic energy market, but not all of them are approved by the regulator **Ofgem**.

Comparison sites make money by getting a commission from the retailer if you make a purchase via their site.

It is no different with energy. If you visit an Energy Comparison site and switch provider, the new supplier will pay the comparison site. At the time of writing that is about £60 for dual fuel (both gas & electricity) and £30 for a single fuel.

So, when you see companies offering to 'take all the hassle' out of switching and making sure you are always on the cheapest tariff, you can see why. They will be paid a commission 'every time' they switch you to a new product.

The reality is, however, that switching is relatively easy and if you do it yourself, via a Cashback website, **you will be paid part of the commission**.

Ofgem only approve Comparison sites if they are satisfied that they show the whole market, without favour of those offering the highest commission.

The below commercial comparison sites are the only ones currently approved by Ofgem:

Energy Helpline	**Energylinx**	The Energy Shop
Money Supermarket	My Utility Genius	**Quotezone**
Runpath	**Simply Switch**	
Switch Gas and Electric	Unravel It	**Uswitch**

Both Quidco and Topcashback receive commission from the retailers when you make a purchase, they share some of this with you as cashback.

The Ofgem approved comparison sites highlighted in bold are the ones that feature on Quidco and/or Topcashback.

Cashback amounts vary, so you have to be alert to ensure you avail yourself of the highest amount.

Both cashback sites also offer their own comparison tool, offering a higher rate of cashback, but these are not Ofgem approved.

Please also be aware that individual Energy suppliers also feature on the cashback sites offering higher cashback rates if you go direct to their website.

Please remember that this is **FREE** money on top of whatever savings you may make by switching supplier.

Please give it a go – what have you got to lose?

Worried about doing this yourself? - Ask someone you trust to help you.

When you are comparing Energy providers and Tariffs, you need to take account of 'Customer Service' rating as well as the cost.

Example (correct as of 1st June 2020)

Prepayment meter customer with SSE (5-star rating) for gas and electricity, spends an average of £40 a month on electricity and £30 a month on gas – **Annual spend of £840.**

Switch to Bulb (4-star rating) Vari-Fair Prepayment – **Annual spend of £720.**

Same usage on a **Credit meter**, pay by monthly direct debit, SSE standard tariff – **Annual spend of £797.**

Switch to Shell Energy (4-star rating) June 2021 v4 Smart Meter (price fixed to 30/06/21 and a new Smart meter installed) – **Annual spend of £566.**

All of the above prices are based on using EXACTLY to same amount of

Gas (6,684kWh) and Electricity (2,102kWh).

So, the same amount of Gas & Electricity can cost you **£840 or £566** depending upon what meter you have and which supplier you use!

Plus, you can get Cashback of up to £42.

How to switch energy provider.

There are many misconceptions about how hard it is to switch energy supplier. For example, some people still believe their cables and pipes have to be replaced or that, if they rent their home they are not allowed to change.

The reality is that when you switch supplier, the only thing that changes is who you pay your money to; and if you are responsible for paying the bills then you can choose your own provider.

That being said, if the switch means a change of meter, your landlord will have to approve it.

In order to switch you will need certain information:

1. The name of your current provider,
2. The name of your current tariff,
3. Your postcode (prices vary dependent upon where you live),
4. Your annual usage or spend,
5. How you would like to pay your new supplier.

Answers for 1 – 4 can be found on your bill or annual statement.

Visit one of the approved comparison websites, preferably via Quidco or Topcashback, but it is your choice.

Normally at the top left of the page you will see an option to select 'all available plans' or 'plans that the comparison site can switch you to'.

If you are relying upon cashback from the comparison site, then you have to switch to one of their options.

Answer the questions as they appear, there will be drop down bars to confirm your supplier and tariff details. Make a note of your annual spend.

At the bottom of the page, click to see how much you can save.

The results page will show you all of your options with the cheapest price first.

At the time of writing, the cheapest tariffs require the fitting of a Smart meter and the opening of an online account.

It is worth checking all plans first before making a decision.

In the example above, a 3-star provider, 'Outfox the Market', came in at **£531.**

NB   If you are currently in receipt of the '*Warm Home Discount*', it is important to check that the supplier you switch to also offers it; as several of the smaller energy companies do not.

If you complete an online or telephone switch, you are covered by the Consumer Contracts Regulations, which automatically gives you a minimum 14 day cooling off period.

This means that you can change your mind without penalty, within a minimum of 14 days from agreeing the switch.

So, if you make an online switch, nothing will happen for the first 14 days. Your new provider will then contact your current provider and they will agree a date for the switch to become effective.

If you are a Credit meter customer you will be asked to provide meter readings in order for your current provider to prepare a final bill and your new provider to start billing you from.

If you pay your current provider by Direct Debit, do not cancel it until the final bill has been agreed.

If you are in credit you will automatically be refunded.

If you are a prepayment customer, your new provider may have to send you a new key and/or card. It is best practice to run down your meter because you may lose any credit balance at the time of the switch.

If you are already on a 'fixed rate' tariff with an early exit fee, you can switch without penalty from 49 days before the tariff end date.

Warm Home Discount

If you qualify, the warm home discount scheme is a payment of £140, credited to your electricity account (can be your gas account if you have same supplier for both).

Most, but not all, energy suppliers, are part of the scheme. If you think you qualify then it is in your interest to be supplied by a provider that makes the payment.

It does not matter if you are a 'Prepayment meter' or 'Credit meter' customer.

There are two ways to qualify: the 'Core group' and the 'Broader group'.

Core Group

At the time of writing, if on 5th July 2020 you are in receipt of the 'guaranteed element of pension credit you will qualify automatically.

Broader Group

Each provider has different criteria, but generally they are based on being in receipt of a means-tested benefits, a member of the household having a disability or being under 6 years old. Some providers simply have an age criteria.

Broader group customers have to apply for the payment, during a 'window of opportunity', that again is different for each supplier.

All suppliers allocate a certain amount of money for the scheme on a first come first served basis.

If you think you qualify, check with your provider, and apply in good time.

At the time of writing the following energy suppliers are fully involved in the scheme:

Avro Energy, Boost, British Gas, Bulb Energy, E(gas and Electricity), E.ON, EDF Energy, Green Network Energy, Green Star Energy, Lumo, npower, npower Select, Octopus Energy, OVO, Powerhouse, Pure Planet, ScottishPower, Shell Energy, So Energy, Spark, SSE, Symbio Energy, Tonik Energy, Utilita and Utility Warehouse.

The following providers partake in the scheme for 'Core Group' customers only:

Angelic Energy, Beam Energy, Bristol Energy, Citizen Energy, Ebico, Ecotricity, Fosse Energy, Great North Energy, Green Energy, iSupply Energy, Ram Energy, Robin Hood Energy, Southend Energy, The LECCY, Utility Point, White Rose Energy and Your Energy Sussex.

How does your usage compare?

Typical Domestic Consumption Values (kWh) Ofgem – 1st April 2020 (medium size house, 3 – 4 people)

	Gas	Electricity
Low	**8,000**	**1,800**
Medium	**12,000**	**2,900**
High	**17,000**	**4,300**

Energy Efficiency

Being more energy efficient will help to reduce your bills by lowering consumption.

You can make some small changes to your lifestyle that will reduce your usage:

- Use energy efficient lightbulbs - LEDs are the most efficient light bulb on the market, they are available with varying degrees of brightness, colours, and 'colour temperatures' – from warm white to cool white in appearance – and can suit almost all light fittings,
- Turn off lights when you leave the room,
- Check your boiler and central heating settings – if your hot water is too hot to touch, turn down the boiler; comfortable room

temperatures are suggested as between 18°C and 21°C, but you may need it warmer if you are elderly or have a health condition,

- Try turning down the thermostat by 1°C, if comfortable try another degree, if you feel cold turn it up again,
- If possible buy energy saving appliances when replacing Washing machines, tumble dryers, dishwashers, cookers and kettles,
- Only fill the kettle with the amount of water needed for the number of people having a drink,
- One full washing machine is cheaper than two half loads,
- Only use a tumble dryer if absolutely essential,
- When cooking, cook more than one meal at a time and freeze the extra meals for another day,
- Switch off standbys,
- If necessary, draught proof windows and doors,
- Showering is cheaper than bathing, but do not dwell in there,
- Fit a water efficient shower head,
- Hang thick curtains to prevent heat escaping through the window, and make sure that they do not cover radiators,
- Do not hide radiators you are using with furniture,

Home energy efficiency improvements to your home, such as insulation and boiler replacement can be expensive, but you may qualify for a free grant or interest free loan.

Availability of grants and loans is dependent upon where you live and who your energy supplier is, each will have different eligibility criteria.

The **Energy Company Obligation (ECO)** is a Government energy efficiency scheme in Great Britain to tackle fuel poverty and help reduce carbon emissions.

The following energy suppliers contribute to the scheme by funding the installation of energy efficiency measures in British households:

Avro Energy, Bristol Energy, British Gas, Bulb, E, E.ON Energy, Ecotricity, EDF Energy, Green Network, Green Star, iSupply, npower, Octopus Energy, OVO, Pure Planet, Robin Hood Energy, Scottish and Southern Energy (SSE), ScottishPower, Shell Energy (formerly First Utility), So Energy, The Co-operative Energy, The Utility Warehouse, Tonik Energy, Utilita and Utility Point.

General eligibility criteria is being in receipt of at least one of the following benefits and satisfy the relevant income requirements, where applicable:

- Armed Forces Independence Payment
- Attendance Allowance
- Carer's Allowance
- Child Benefit (on the condition that the household's relevant income does not exceed the amount set out in Chapter 3 of our scheme guidance)
- Constant Attendance Allowance
- Disability Living Allowance
- Pension Guarantee Credit
- Income-related Employment and Support Allowance (ESA)
- Income-based Jobseeker's Allowance (JSA)

- Income Support

- Industrial Injuries Disablement Benefit

- Mobility Supplement

- Personal Independence Payment

- Severe Disablement Allowance

- Tax Credits (Child Tax Credits and Working Tax Credits)

- Universal Credit

Contact your energy supplier for more information.

To check the availability of grants/loans in your locality use the below link and enter your postcode.

https://www.simpleenergyadvice.org.uk/grants

Wales

If you live in Wales you may qualify for free energy efficiency home improvements, such as a new boiler, central heating, or insulation, funded by Welsh Government under the **'Nest'** scheme.

You could be eligible for free home energy efficiency improvements if:

- You own or privately rent your home
- Your home is energy inefficient and expensive to heat
- You or someone you live with receives a means tested benefit OR has a chronic respiratory, circulatory or mental health condition and an income below the defined thresholds

The means tested benefits that qualify are:

- Child Tax Credit (income below £16,105 a year)
- Council Tax Reduction (exemption and discount do not qualify on their own)
- Housing Benefit
- Income-based Jobseeker's Allowance
- Income-related Employment and Support Allowance
- Income Support
- Pension Credit
- Universal Credit
- Working Tax Credit (income below £16,105 a year)

Health Eligibility Criteria

Someone in the home must:

- Be living with a chronic respiratory, circulatory or mental health condition. These include:
    - Respiratory disease (respiratory infections, broncho-constriction in asthma, and chronic obstructive pulmonary disease)
    - Circulatory disease (including cardio-vascular disease, strokes and heart attacks)
    - Mental health issues (including depression, anxiety, psychosis and bipolar disorders, dementia, intellectual and development disorders).
- Be living on a low income below the defined thresholds

For more information Call Freephone 0808 808 2244.

Scotland

If you live in Scotland, you may qualify for free energy efficiency home improvements funded by Scottish Government under the **'Warmer Homes Scotland Scheme'**.

Warmer Homes Scotland is designed to help vulnerable people make their homes warmer and more comfortable by installing a range of energy saving measures, including Wall insulation, Loft insulation, Draught-proofing, Central heating and Renewables.

To qualify for Warmer Homes Scotland the household must meet all of the following criteria:

- Be homeowners or the tenants of a private-sector landlord
- Live in the home as their main residence
- Have lived there for at least 12 months (unless in receipt of a DS1500 certificate)
- Live in home with an energy rating of 67 or lower and which is not more than 230 square metres in floor size
- Live in a home that meets the tolerable living standard set out in the Housing (Scotland) Act 2006 or, where the home does not meet the tolerable living standards, this will not impact on the effectiveness of the measures recommended for installation under the scheme
- Householders must not have received support for energy efficiency measures through Warmer Homes Scotland or HEEPS ABS funding in the last five years.

Plus meet one of the following conditions

- Be of pensionable age, have no working heating system and be in receipt of a passport benefit
- Be aged over 75 and in receipt of a passport benefit
- Pregnant and/or have a child under 16 and in receipt of a passport benefit
- Have a disability and be in receipt of any level of Personal Independent Payment (PIP)
- Have a disability and be in receipt of high rate Disability Living Allowance (DLA) (care or mobility component)
- Have a disability and be in receipt of low/medium rate Disability Living Allowance (DLA) (care or mobility component) and be in receipt of an income related benefit
- Be a carer in receipt of Carers Allowance
- Have been injured or disabled serving in the Armed Forces and be in receipt of Armed Forces Independence Payment/War Disablement Pension
- Have an injury or disability from an accident or disease caused by work and be in receipt of Industrial Injuries Disablement Benefit.

The passport benefits are:

- Guarantee element of the Pension Credit
- Attendance Allowance
- Universal Credit or any of the benefits due to be replaced by Universal Credit (Income Based JSA, Child Tax Credit, Working Tax Credit, Employment and Support Allowance, Income Support, Housing Benefit)
- Council Tax Reduction (excluding 25% discount for single occupancy)
- Carer's Allowance
- Higher Rate Care or Mobility components of Disability Living Allowance (DLA) or Personal Independence Payment (PIP)
- Armed Forces Independence Payment
- War Disablement Pension
- Industrial Injuries Disablement Benefit.

For more information about the scheme, contact Home Energy Scotland on 0808 808 228.

Northern Ireland

Energy Saving Trust NI manages the Northern Ireland Sustainable Energy Programme (NISEP) on behalf of the Utility Regulator. NISEP provides grants to help you implement energy-saving measures in your home, such as grants for energy-efficient boilers, heating, loft insulation and cavity wall insulation.

It provides approx. £8 million of funding for energy efficiency work in NI each year. Primary Bidders to this scheme have designed a range of offers and incentives for those people who fall outside of other government funded schemes. Visit the Utility Regulator for a current list of schemes.

Affordable Warmth

Affordable Warmth is funded by the Department for Social Development. If you are an owner occupier or householder of a privately rented property and your gross annual household income is less than £20,000 you may be eligible for a package of energy-efficiency and heating measures, tailored to each household.

Householders should contact their Local Council to enquire about Affordable Warmth.

Boiler Replacement Scheme

The scheme, provided by funding from the Northern Ireland Executive, offers owner occupiers a grant of up to £1,000 to:

- Replace inefficient boilers with energy-efficient condensing oil or gas boilers.
- Switch from oil to gas.
- Switch to a wood pellet boiler.

It is available to those who earn less than £40,000 a year with an inefficient boiler of at least 15 years and is dependent on total gross income. The scheme, administered by the Northern Ireland Housing Executive (NIHE), is targeted at householders who do not qualify for other Government energy-efficient improvement schemes, making them vulnerable to fuel poverty.

For more information call 0300 200 7874.

Cold Weather Payment

You may qualify for a Cold Weather Payment, if between 1 November and 31 March, you are in receipt of: Pension Credit, Income Support, Income-based Jobseeker's Allowance, Income-related Employment and Support Allowance, Universal Credit or Support for Mortgage Interest.

If you qualify, you will automatically receive £25 for each 7-day period that the average temperature in your area is recorded as, or forecast to be, zero degrees celsius or below over 7 consecutive days.

Cold Weather Payments do not affect your other benefits.

Winter Fuel Payment

The Winter Fuel Payment is a payment of between £100 and £300 to help towards your winter heating bills.

Most payments are made automatically between November and December and are usually paid by mid-January at the latest.

How much you will get depends on your circumstances. Any money you receive is tax-free and will not affect your other benefits.

At the time of writing, you qualify for a Winter Fuel Payment if both the following apply:

- you were born on or before 5 October 1954
- you lived in the UK for at least one day during the week of 21 to 27 September 2020 - this is called the 'qualifying week'

You cannot get the payment if you live in Cyprus, France, Gibraltar, Greece, Malta, Portugal or Spain because the average winter temperature is higher than the warmest region of the UK.

How much you get depends on your circumstances during the qualifying week.

If you receive certain benefits

Your payment may be different if you or your partner get one of the following benefits:

- Pension Credit
- income-based Jobseeker's Allowance (JSA)
- income-related Employment and Support Allowance (ESA)
- Income Support

Contact your local Citizens Advice for further information.

Water Rates (correct as of 2nd June 2020)

There are nine Private Water & Sewerage Companies in England and one 'not for profit' Company in Wales, who operate on a geographical basis.

Anglian Water, Dwr Cymru Welsh Water, Northumbrian Water, Severn Trent Water, South West Water, Southern Water, Thames Water, United Utilities, Wessex Water and Yorkshire Water.

Scottish Water and Northern Ireland Water are run by the public sector.

Social Tariff

Every Water & Sewerage company in England & Wales has a social tariff for customers on low incomes. They all have different names: Assist, Lite, Big Difference, Essentials, Watercare, Watersure Plus, Help to Pay, Help-U, Water support, and SupportPLUS, each with different eligibility criteria.

If you qualify, your rates are capped to an annual amount between £211 and £408 or up to 90% of your annual bill, dependent upon where you live.

General eligibility rules in relation to household income, number of persons in household and receipt of income related benefits.

The below link will take you to webpage that includes information on all Social Tariff schemes.

https://www.ccwater.org.uk/households/help-with-my-bills/

Water meters

If you do not have a water meter you will be charged the unmetered rate, regardless of how much water your household uses. This cost varies between companies, so again, is dependent upon where you live.

If you have a water meter, you will only pay for what you use. Generally, households of three people or less, will save money by being metered. It may also be worth considering if your un-metered bills are based on the rateable value of your home.

Meters will be installed free of charge and you will normally be allowed a trial period of up to 2 years, to ensure that the installation was cost effective.

If you think you would benefit from a water meter – contact your supplier.

Watersure

This is a scheme which caps the bill for customers with a water meter, who have a large family or a member of the household living with a medical condition that requires the use of a lot of water. The amount of the cap varies between companies, but eligibility is broadly the same:

A member of the household in receipt of one of the below benefits:

- universal credit,
- income support,
- housing benefit,

- pension credit,
- income-based jobseeker's allowance,
- working tax credit,
- income-related employment and support allowance,
- child tax credit (except families in receipt of the family element only).

You will then also need to either:

- be in receipt of child benefit for 3 or more children under 19 living in the household or
- have, (or have someone living with you who has) one of the following medical conditions:
    - desquamation, (flaky skin loss),
    - weeping skin disease, (eczema, psoriasis, varicose ulceration),
    - incontinence,
    - abdominal stoma,
    - Crohn's disease,
    - ulcerative colitis,
    - renal failure requiring dialysis at home (where there is no contribution by the local health authority for the cost of the water used).

And as a result of that condition the person affected is obliged to use a significant additional volume of water.

Additionally, where a doctor certifies (by the provision of a certificate) that you, or someone living with you need to use a significant amount of additional water because of any other medical condition you may qualify for the capped bill.

If you think you are eligible for the Social Tariff or Watersure, please contact your water company or visit your local Citizens Advice for assistance.

Chapter Four

Bank Accounts, Saving & Borrowing

Financial Inclusion

Financial capability advisers have striven for years to empower their learners with the skills and knowledge to avail themselves of the best available financial products for their circumstances.

Unfortunately, not all financial products are universally available, and it is a sad reflection of our society that the cheapest products are generally only available to those with the highest credit scores and/or highest incomes.

That being said, this section is designed to assist you to identify what is best for you and how you can improve your chances of getting a better deal.

Financial terms that are useful to know.

- **Credit Rating**
- **Interest rate**
- **Annual Percentage Rate (APR)**
- **Financial Conduct Authority (FCA)**

Credit Rating

Your credit rating, (also known as credit score), is what lenders use to assess the risk you pose as an individual applying for credit. It is based upon their prediction of your ability to repay a debt based on your previous actions.

Not all lenders have the same criteria, but they will apply similar tests to identify your suitability for their financial product.

Equifax, Experian, and TransUnion (previously Callcredit).

There are three UK credit reference agencies that compile our financial information and all lenders use at least one of them. The data they use comes from five main sources:

1. Electoral roll – public documents containing names and addresses.
2. Court records – public documents containing information on County Court Judgements (CCJs), Decrees, IVAs, Bankruptcies and other court debt orders.
3. Search, address, and linked data - records of previous credit applications and searches made by other lenders, addresses you are linked to and names of other people you have a financial association with.
4. Account data – a six-year record of your account behaviour in respect of bank / building society accounts, energy contracts, credit / store cards, loans, mortgages, and mobile phone contracts.
5. Fraud data – details of any convictions for fraud in your name.

It is vitally important that you do everything possible to build a positive credit score and maintain it.

The first thing to do is to check what your current rating is. You can apply to all three credit reference agencies for a FREE report.

You can apply by following the information in the below links:

https://www.moneysavingexpert.com/creditclub/

Joining the MoneySavingExpert club will allow you to access your free Experian report plus take advantage of many more money saving tips, including their 'cheap energy club'.

https://www.clearscore.com/?utm_source=mse&utm_medium=site&utm_campaign=mse-site

Joining Clearscore will give you free access to your Equifax report.

https://www.creditkarma.co.uk/

Joining CreditKarma will give you free access to your TransUnion report.

It is important to check your report for accuracy. If you identify something that you think is wrong, challenge it.

Tips for improving your credit score

- Make sure you are registered on the Electoral register at your current address,

- If you are not eligible to be included on the Electoral register (mainly foreign Nationals) – send all three credit agencies proof of residence and ask them to add a note to your profile,

- Don't be late or miss a credit repayment – paying bills on time will boost your score,

- Try not to be financially linked to someone with a poor rating – if your spouse/partner/flatmate has a poor score it will pay you to keep your finances totally separate,

- If your relationship breaks down, make sure that all financial ties are severed. You can ask the credit agencies for a 'Notice of Disassociation',

- Minimise credit applications by using a free eligibility calculator. These are readily available online, the tools on https://www.moneysavingexpert.com are very user friendly,

- Check that all of your accounts and driving documents show your current address, if they do not – change them,

- Do not make multiple applications for credit in quick succession,

- Credit cards can be a recipe for disaster – but if you are disciplined, it pays to apply for a Credit card with a **low credit limit** and set up a direct debit to **repay it in full every month**. Only use it for things like groceries and fuel – and ensure that you have enough money to clear the debt every month. **If you cannot trust yourself to do this, then stay away from them,**
- Never withdraw cash on a credit card – it gives the impression that you are desperate,
- Time applications right – court records last for six years, data about previous applications for one year. Check your file and if some of the history is due to be expunged, wait until it has gone,
- Do not take out high interest loans – again it gives the impression of desperation.

Interest Rate

Saving - the interest rate is the return received on an investment and is normally shown as a % figure.

Borrowing – the interest rate is the cost of borrowing money, normally shown as a % of the amount borrowed.

The interest rate for savers is usually lower than the rate for borrowers.

Annual Percentage Rate

Annual percentage rate (APR) is the official rate used to help you understand and compare the annual cost of borrowing. It takes into account the interest rate and additional charges of a credit offer. All lenders have to tell you what their APR is before you sign a credit agreement.

APR is expressed as a percentage of the amount you have borrowed. For example, a personal loan with a 15% APR should be cheaper than one with a 17.5% APR, although you should always check the terms and conditions.

It is worth noting that APR only includes compulsory charges. Some fees, such as payment protection, may not be considered, so you should always read the terms and conditions carefully before applying for credit.

Representative APR

The representative APR is an advertised rate that at least 51% of those accepted for the credit deal will get. That means that almost half the people who are approved for the deal may not be eligible for the advertised rate and will have to pay more.

Personal APR

A personal APR is the rate you are actually given, this could be the same as the representative rate, or it could be higher, depending on your circumstances. The lender will usually decide what rate to offer you based on how your credit and financial information matches their criteria.

As a general rule, with a loan, the more you borrow, the lower the APR is likely to be. With credit cards, rates often vary from around 5% to over 30% - the rate you are offered usually depends on how high your credit score is. It is worth noting that these rates are usually based on rates for making purchases (e.g. online or instore). Rates for other transactions, such as cash withdrawals, may be different.

Financial Conduct Authority

The Financial Conduct Authority (FCA) regulates the financial services industry in the UK. Its role includes protecting consumers, keeping the industry stable, and promoting healthy competition between financial service providers.

Bank Accounts

Current accounts, usually with a bank or building society, are used by most people in order to manage their day-to-day income and expenditure.

With a current account you can:

- set up a Direct Debit or standing order to make regular payments,

- receive payments such as salary, wages, or benefits,

- have access to an authorised overdraft,

- have a debit card, which can be used to make purchase and withdraw cash from ATMs.

There are two main types of current account:

1. **Basic accounts** are free; however, you cannot have an overdraft facility, but you will get a debit card and can set up direct debits and standing orders.

2. **Packaged accounts** have a monthly fee, which varies according to the features of the account. You get a debit card, can agree an overdraft facility, set up direct debits and standing orders. There are several different types of packaged account, so it is especially important that you weigh up the cost against the services on offer before you sign up to one.

Packaged accounts may pay you interest on your balance, or pay you cashback on the direct debits you set up or provide free insurance; but invariably these require a certain amount of money to be paid in each month.

If you are considering opening a packaged account, or switching to a new one, the below link is a good comparison tool:

https://www.moneysavingexpert.com/banking/compare-best-bank-accounts/

You might also want to ask yourself:

- How many of the extras do I really need?

- Could I get the services separately for less?

- Does the insurance give me the right amount of cover?

- Do I already have cover through another product? For example, do you have cover through your home insurance policy.

A **Post Office Card account** is a free account, generally used by people who have not got a bank account; but can only be used for the receipt of money from HM Government Departments e.g. pension, benefits, and tax credits. You cannot pay other money (cash / cheques) into your account. You can only withdraw cash from a Post Office branch, or a Post Office branded ATM. Your card is not a debit card or payment card and it cannot be used to pay for things. You cannot have an overdraft, nor set up direct debits and standing orders.

Savings Accounts

As part of your budgeting plan, you should always try to allocate some of your income for regular savings. I know that this may be difficult, but it is a good habit to get into.

There is a wide choice of savings accounts, so you need to do some research to find the best product for you.

What are you saving for?

You can use different savings accounts for different reasons. If you are saving for that 'rainy day', you should use an instant access account; but if saving for a deposit to buy your own home, then a fixed-rate account may be more suitable.

Are you looking at saving a specific amount, or are you looking at a specific time period? Can you save a regular amount each month, or will you add to the pot as and when you can?

Your answers will help to identify which account is best for you, then you need to find the provider offering the best rates of interest.

Comparing interest rates.

Not all savings accounts have the same interest rates. Some providers will try and entice you with introductory offers but remember that this rate will be time limited.

Are you savvy enough to keep switching provider to avail yourself of the best deals?

If not, then you should look long term and go with the provider offering the best standard rate.

It is easier to use a Comparison website, rather than trawl through individual providers' websites.

I can recommend the link below, but there are others out there.

https://www.moneysavingexpert.com/banking/?tab=sect7

Help to save scheme.

This is a Government scheme, designed for working people living in low income households.

To qualify you must be earning a wage **and** claiming Universal Credit or Working Tax Credit.

The scheme pays out 50 pence for every £1.00 saved over a four-year period, up to a maximum of £1,200. The payments are paid as 'tax free bonuses' directly into your bank account.

You can save between £1 and £50 each month, but you do not have to save every month.

The 'bonuses' are paid in two instalments, the first after 2 years and the second at the end of the four years period.

The first bonus is calculated on the 'highest' balance that was in your account during the first two years.

Example 1.   You save £40 a month and make no withdrawals, at the end of 2 years you will have saved £960, your bonus will be £480 (50% of £960).

Example 2.   You save £50 a month for the whole of year one and ten months of year two, a total of £1,100, but have to withdraw £400 in the eleventh month to buy a new washing machine. You manage to save another £50 in the final month of the 2-year period. At the end of the 2nd year, your balance will be £750. Your bonus will be calculated on the highest balance that was in your account during the 2-year period, so your bonus will be £550 (50% of £1,100).

The second bonus, paid when your account closes after four years, will be calculated on the difference between the highest balance in years 1 & 2 and the highest balance during years 3 & 4.

Example 3.   You save £40 a month every month for 2 years, making no withdrawals. In years 1 & 2, you saved £960 and received a bonus of £480 that was paid into your bank account. During years 3 & 4, you save £30 every month, again making no withdrawals. At the end of year 4, your balance is £1,680, your final bonus is calculated by subtracting £960 from £1,680, which is £720. Your second bonus will be 50% of £720, which is £360.

Example 4.   In years 1 & 2, you saved £1,150, but withdrew £400 to buy the washing machine. Your highest balance was £1,100 and you received your bonus of £550. During years 3 & 4 you manage to save £40 every month and make no withdrawals. At the end of the 4-year period your final balance is £750 + £960, which is £1,710. Your 2nd bonus is calculated by subtracting £1,100 from £1,710, which is £610, giving a bonus of £305.

So, just to be clear, in example 4, even though you saved £960 in years 3 & 4, your bonus will be £305 and not £480 (50% of the £960 paid in).

If your highest balance during years 3 & 4 is less or equal to the highest balance of years 1 & 2, then you will not receive a second bonus.

Your account will close, 4 years from the date of opening. You can withdraw money at any time. If you close the account before the 4-year anniversary, you will not get the 2nd bonus.

To open a 'Help to save' account you can call HMRC on **0300 322 7093**, or click the below link:

https://www.gov.uk/get-help-savings-low-income/how-to-apply

Alternatively, you may want to consider Premium Bonds.

Premium Bonds are issued by National Savings and Investment (NS&I).

They are a type of raffle ticket, where you are entered into a monthly prize draw, but you never lose your stake money. Prizes are between £25 and £1 million tax free.

The minimum investment is £25, which remains your money and can be withdrawn at any time. The amount of your investment will remain the same, but its value will decrease each year because of inflation.

• the maximum holding for one individual is currently £50,000.

• for each £1 saved you get a unique bond number, each one is a ticket for the monthly draw. You will be entered into every monthly draw, starting a full month after purchase, until you take your investment out.

• anyone aged 16 or over can buy premium bonds for themselves, but you also them on behalf of your child, grandchild, or great-grandchild..

Premium bonds might not be for you if you need a guaranteed, regular income from your investment.

Credit Unions

Credit unions are community banks, set up by and for members to benefit their specific community.

They mainly offer savings accounts and loans to their members, but some now offer current accounts too.

Credit union current accounts offer different services, so what is available will depend on which credit union you use. Most are free, but some may charge an administration fee.

Most credit union current accounts:

- let you pay cheques in for free,
- allow you to pay money in at their office or at a collection point,
- have the facility for wages, benefits, pensions, and tax credits to be paid straight into your account,
- let you withdraw money out from their office, collection point or specific ATMs,
- let you set up Direct Debits and standing orders,
- offer a pre-paid card or a debit card to allow you to make purchases,
- organise budgeting sections in your account for different types of expenditure.

Whichever credit union you use, there is no minimum monthly amount you have to pay into your current account.

You also will not need to pass a credit check to get an account, because credit unions do not usually offer overdrafts.

If you need to borrow money, you can apply to the credit union for a loan.

To become a member of a credit union, you need to have a common bond with the other members. This is normally that you live in a certain area or work for a specific employer; but it can also include membership of an organisation.

Savings accounts

One of the main reasons for joining a Credit Union, is to save money. You can save whatever you can whenever you can afford to do it. The investments do not have to be regular, but it is a great habit to get into. You can also open accounts for your children and is a good way to teach them the value of money.

Once you have joined and been saving with the credit union for a certain period of time, you can apply for a loan.

Loans

Credit unions are governed by the same rules as Banks and Building Societies. They should only lend money to members that can afford to pay them back; but the local nature of a Credit Union allows for human judgements not computerised ones. Still, assessments have to made based on savings history, current income, and other expenditure.

Currently interest is capped at 3% a month in Great Britain and 1% a month in Northern Ireland.

To find your nearest Credit Union use the following link:

https://www.findyourcreditunion.co.uk/

We have looked at some different options for how to save, but as previously identified you need to know what you are saving for, in order to make an informed choice of how you save, especially in relation to having access to your money.

Reasons for saving:

- Emergencies
- Retirement
- Deposit for a house
- Holiday
- Car
- Babies/Children
- Christmas and Birthday presents
- New furniture
- New TV/ Games Consoles/ DVD
- Cooker/ Fridge/ Freezer

This is not an exhaustive list, but you can see that some are short-term, others mid-term and long-term; they all require different planning and prioritising.

Save as much as you can for as long as you are able to.

Borrowing

Most people will need to borrow money at some stage, to tide them over in an emergency, to buy larger items or to fund a special event. Before you borrow money, it is important to make sure you will be able to keep up the repayments.

Depending on the reason for your borrowing, you need to consider your options:

- Use Savings
- Hire Purchase (interest Free)
- Personal Loan – **Beware of loan sharks**
- Family/Friends
- Overdraft
- Credit Card (Interest free)

Use savings

If you have enough savings to cover the amount you are considering borrowing, then you need to compare the interest rates of what you are earning on the savings against what you will be paying on a loan.

Hire Purchase

Generally, stores and catalogues charge very high interest rates on their HP products. **Remember to check the APR.**

However occasionally they offer 0% APR or 'buy now pay later' deals.

0% APR deals are always attractive, as no interest or fees are charged, and you can spread payments rather than pay a lump sum all in one go. If you can manage the repayments then you should consider this option.

If you have the cash to buy something, but there is a 'buy now pay later deal' available; why not invest the money in Premium Bonds and cash them in just before the payment has to be made. It is important to set a reminder for the cashing in, because if you do not pay in accordance with the offer you could be liable for high interest and/or charges.

Personal Loan

Personal loans are either secured or unsecured.

Secured loans generally have a lower APR, but you need to be homeowner and allow the lender to have a charge against it.

Do not confuse a secured loan with a mortgage.

Mortgage rates are generally lower, and it may be better for you to re-mortgage, rather than take a second charge out against your home.

The repayment term for a secured loan can be up to 40 years depending on your circumstances.

NB - if you default on payments you may lose your home.

Unsecured loans do not require a security and are generally for shorter periods of 1 – 5 years. It may be possible to get a loan for up to 10 years.

You can apply for a personal loan from a number of lenders. It is important to do some research first; when comparing, use the **APR** to identify the cheapest deals, but always check for extortionate penalty fees for late payments.

Use an eligibility checker to identify your suitability before making an application. If you are declined, this may leave a negative marker on your credit score.

Banks and Building Societies normally offer the lowest APR, but they also carry out the strictest checks on your suitability. If they decline your application it is because they do not think that you can afford the repayments.

Do not fall into the trap of resorting to high interest lenders, who have a more relaxed lending criteria. You could be trapped for a very long time repaying a relatively small loan because of interest charges and fees.

If you are on a low income, I strongly recommend that you join a Credit Union and when you need a loan, they will give you a fair deal.

Loan Sharks are criminals who prey on the vulnerable, avoid at all costs.

Generally, a loan shark, or illegal money lender will:

- be very eager to 'do you a favour' and lend whatever you need, with little discussion about how much you have to pay back,
- probably not give you any paperwork, such as a credit agreement,
- be vague at best, in relation to interest rates or what your balance is,
- add additional charges at any time,
- when it suits, may explain that you "will be paying for a very long time", but "can always borrow more if you need to",
- demand identity documents, or bank cards 'as security',
- make it very difficult to settle your debt,
- get nasty if you do not play ball. This will normally be in the form of threats of violence or to you and your family but may be more subtle threats if they have a different hold over you.

If you are worried that you are involved with a loan shark, you should report it.

England   https://www.stoploansharks.co.uk/

0300 555 2222

Wales   email: imlu@cardiff.gov.uk

0300 123 3311

Scotland   https://www.tsscot.co.uk/report-a-

consumer-issue/   **0800 074 0878**

Northern Ireland

https://www.nidirect.gov.uk/information-and-services/government-citizens-and-rights/consumer-advice

0300 123 6262

Family / Friends

If you are fortunate enough to have family members or close friends that are in a position to lend you money, then this is an option to consider.

Be careful though, arrangements like this, no matter how informal, may cause friction down the line if you are unable to repay the debt.

Overdraft

If you have an agreed overdraft facility on your current account, this may the cheapest way to borrow money on a **short-term** basis. **Do not** go beyond the agreed limit, it could prove very expensive.

If you cannot clear your overdraft within a couple of months, you may be better off applying for a personal loan with a lower APR.

Credit Cards

If your credit rating is good enough you may be eligible for a credit card that offers an introductory 0% APR on purchases. Use an eligibility checker to identify the cards you may qualify for and go for the one with the longest 0% period.

It is essential that you repay the amount advanced within the specified time otherwise you will incur high interest rates.

Calculate if you can afford to do this by dividing the amount borrowed by the number of months of 0% offered. If it is affordable, set up a Direct Debit for at least that amount to ensure it is paid off.

Do not use the credit card for other purchases. When the offer period is over and the loan paid off, consider closing the account.

Do not be tempted to hold on to credit cards if you are not using them.

The total amount of credit available to you, even if your balance is £0.00, will have a negative impact on your credit score.

and finally, a few extra things to consider

White Goods

If you need a new washing machine, fridge or cooker and you are on a low income, you may be eligible for a charitable grant.

You can use the grant checker at

https://grants-search.turn2us.org.uk/

You can also seek advice from your local **Citizens Advice**.

Grants are not loans and do not have to be repaid.

Mortgages

If you have a mortgage, it is wise to review your borrowing on a regular basis. You may be able to find a cheaper mortgage deal with another lender. You may have to pay charges for changing your mortgage lender, especially if you are leaving before the fixed term expiry date.

You can get more information about switching your mortgage from the Money Advice Service.

https://www.moneyadviceservice.org.uk/en/articles/remortgaging-to-cut-costs

You can compare mortgage products using the following link:

https://www.moneysavingexpert.com/mortgages/best-buys

If you think you would benefit from talking to an Independent Financial Advisor, then a recommendation from someone you trust is usually a good place to start.

If this does not work for you, then the following organisations can help you find an independent financial adviser:

Independent Financial Promotions (IFAP)

Website: www.unbiased.co.uk

Institute of Financial Planning (IFP)

E-mail: enquiries@financialplanning.org.uk

Website: www.financialplanning.org.uk

Personal Finance Society (PFS)

E-mail: customer.serv@thepfs.org

Website: www.findanadviser.org

If you are struggling to pay your mortgage, you must take action quickly to stop yourself from falling into problem debt.

Speak to your lender. You could ask them to reduce your monthly payments, usually for a limited period of time. This might get you over a rough patch and stop a debt from building up. If a debt has already built up, you will need to find a way to clear the debt as well.

Before you agree to make any changes to your mortgage, you should ask your lender if there will be any additional charges and factor them in.

Depending on the type of mortgage you have, you may also be able to change to interest-only payments, even for a short period. You could also consider extending the length of the mortgage; however, this is not a temporary fix and will result in you paying more in the long term.

If you get into debt and your lender thinks you are not dealing with the problem, they may take action through the courts. This could result in you losing your home.

If you are having serious difficulties paying your mortgage, for example, if you have started getting letters from your mortgage lender threatening court action, you should get help from a **specialist debt adviser**.

Cooking on a budget

If you need to reduce your grocery bill, you should be careful to do so properly. It is all too easy to end up eating low quality frozen food. Here are some tips for eating on a budget:

1. Write a shopping list. Plan your meals in advance and buy the exact ingredients you need.

2. Eat your leftovers.

3. Buy frozen fruit and vegetables. Frozen fruit and vegetables are massively underrated. They come pre-chopped and are just as good for you as non-frozen food (but avoid frozen food with added salt, sugar, or fat)

4. Trade down a brand. Switch from premium brands to basic brands and buy unbranded vegetables sold by weight.

5. Pulses, beans, lentils, and peas are budget, healthy and packed with protein, fibre, vitamins, and minerals.

6. Freeze leftover bread. Bread is the most wasted household food. You know you can freeze and toast it?

7. Buy budget cuts of meat, they may lack the style of premium cuts, but they can be just as tasty.

8. Work to a recipe. Consider the price of ingredients when making your recipes. Build a collection of budget foods that you enjoy cooking and eating.

9. Learn portion control. Use smaller plates or add smaller portions to the plate and learn to say no to a second helping. Save the leftovers for lunch.

10. Learn to cook from scratch. Avoiding takeaways and processed ready cook meals can save you a fortune and should reduce your salt and sugar intake.

11. Buy whole chickens. Some of the best-value meat in the supermarket is a whole chicken, which you can easily cut up into regular portions. You can turn chicken bones into an amazing tasting chicken stock.

12. Price-check packaged fruit and vegetables against loose veg. You can save a lot of money by buying loose vegetables.

13. Cut back on luxuries. Try to reduce the number of treats like fizzy drinks, crisps, and biscuits you buy. Save money & improve your health.

14. Beware of BOGOF (Buy One Get One Free) offers. It is not cheaper if you were not planning on getting it in the first place.

15. Cook for your toddler. Blend or chop up their portion to suit their age and freeze extra child-sized portions for later.

16. Shop around. You do not owe any loyalty to a supermarket. Also consider buying from your local fruit and vegetable shops.

17. Most supermarkets discount fresh items towards the end of the day. As a general rule: shopping very late (or very early) is the best way to save money at the supermarket.

18. Cook in bulk. Batch cooking is not just a money saver - it is a time saver, too. By making three litres of a tomato base sauce at a time, with loads of veg grated in; it is the equivalent of six jars of pasta sauce and costs about £1 to make. If you freeze it in portions, it becomes lasagne sauce, pasta sauce, chilli, pizza topping, and even a delicious tomato soup if you water it down.

Some useful websites for recipes:

https://www.bbcgoodfood.com/recipes/collection/cheap-cut

https://www.netmums.com/life/guide-to-cooking-on-a-budget

https://skintdad.co.uk/budget-recipes-easy-meals/

https://www.bbcgoodfood.com/recipes/collection/budget

http://allrecipes.co.uk/recipes/budget-recipes.aspx

https://www.bbcgoodfood.com/recipes/collection/cheap-and-healthy

Christmas on a Budget

Many families struggle financially with Christmas. We all want to give our families the best time we can at Christmas, but so many people rely on credit to pay for it.

Hopefully, by putting into practice some of the things I have already mentioned you will have budgeted for the festivities.

Plan for an affordable Xmas, not one day of decadence followed by months of regret.

Here are some ideas you might want to consider:

1. Set yourself a budget – and stick to it!
2. When considering the purchase of presents, be aware of the 'Black Friday' and 'Cyber Monday' deals. They are high profile to tempt you to 'buy now' ready for Christmas. Remember that goods may be even cheaper in the 'January sales'. Consider giving an IOU for the gift and buy it in January.
3. Ask for a 'gift receipt'.

4. Think about who you are buying for. Some families/friends buy for each other's children, when a little discussion will reveal that no-one can really afford to do it.

5. Home-made gifts – these are often cheaper and show a lot of thought and effort.

6. Personalised gifts – why not try a personalised calendar, framed photo, or a Christmas cheque?

7. How about giving a gift for the family? Board games, puzzles or a big tin of sweets are often an inexpensive option and loved by everyone.

8. Gifts wrapped with plain brown paper and tied with ribbon look great. Alternatively decorate plain paper with unique designs using potato prints.

9. Look around your home and garden for decorations. Bundles of cinnamon sticks tied with twine look great as tree decorations as do biscuits wrapped in silver foil.

10. Share the cost – and the fun – of Christmas dinner. If you are having friends and family over, ask them to buy and prepare a dish to bring to the table.

11. Do not be tempted by luxury brands - look beyond the packaging.

12. Plan what to buy and when – some things are best paid for early to get the best deal and others best to leave until the last minute.

13. Do not forget to factor in delivery costs – try and consolidate your shopping to get the best delivery prices.

14. Search for discounts such as vouchers in magazines and voucher codes online. If there is space on the online checkout to enter a discount code, always search for one.

15. Plan your food list wisely – a bigger turkey will cost more but it is worth it if you can use the leftovers wisely.

16. Compare prices of different retailers via the internet to get the best deal.

17. Payday loans may seem like a good way of getting your hands-on cash quicker than you otherwise would, but beware – the interest rates charged are often very high.

18. You may want to arrange an overdraft on your current account. Talk to your bank in advance and agree an amount – ask for interest-free. Be careful to stick to your agreed limit because if you go over it you will incur charges.

19. Store cards are like credit cards, but you can usually only use them in that store or group of stores. They often promise a discount off whatever you are buying. This can save you money, but store cards tend to charge higher interest rates than most other loans so make sure you will be able to pay off the balance when the first bill comes in.

20. **Start thinking about next Christmas in January!! Join a Credit Union, make regular savings, and do not touch them!**

Gift Vouchers

If you are considering giving gift cards or vouchers, there are two things you should be mindful of:

Sometimes retailers go bust. A host of big-name retailers have gone into administration in recent years. When this happens, they usually stop accepting cards.

Gift cards have expiry dates. Most gift cards must be redeemed within a certain period of time, so the recipient needs to spend them before time runs out.

Pay by Credit Card if the item costs more than £100 and you can afford to pay it off.

If the firm goes bust, or goods do not arrive, or are faulty, it can be a nightmare. However, if you use a credit card (not debit card, cheque or cash) to pay even partly for something costing between £100 and £30,000, the card company is jointly liable for the whole amount.

This protection does not apply to purchases **under £100**, but there is still an option which can help if you use a Visa, Mastercard or Amex credit card, or any debit or charge card. If the goods don't appear or are faulty, you can ask your bank/card provider to reclaim the cash from the seller's bank, so long as you start the chargeback process within 120 days of realising there's a problem.

Thanks for reading.

I hope that the content of this guidebook has helped you to develop your own strategies to take control of your finances.

Good luck.

Printed in Poland
by Amazon Fulfillment
Poland Sp. z o.o., Wrocław